BAKER'S
POCKET
ATLAS
OF THE BIBLE

BAKER'S
POCKET
ATLAS
OF THE BIBLE

Charles F. Pfeiffer

BAKER BOOK HOUSE
Grand Rapids, Michigan

CONTENTS

List of Maps

Color Maps
by
Hammond Incorporated

List of Illustrations

Illustration Credits

1

THE WORLD OF THE BIBLE

The events of Biblical history took place in the lands of the eastern Mediterranean and the area known as the Fertile Crescent. The Fertile Crescent is the name given to the agriculturally productive area that stretches northwestward from the Persian Gulf through the ancient lands of Sumer, Akkad, Babylonia, and Assyria to Syria, after which it extends southwestward through Syria and Palestine into Egypt. On a map of the contemporary Middle East, the countries of the Fertile Crescent, beginning at the Persian Gulf, include Iraq, Syria, southern Turkey, Lebanon, and Israel. On some maps of the Arabian Peninsula, this area appears as a crescent-shaped strip of land north of the Arabian Desert.

The two rivers that provide fertility to the northern and eastern parts of the Fertile Crescent are mentioned in the Biblical account of the Garden of Eden. The Tigris and the Euphrates (Gen. 2:14) flow in their separate

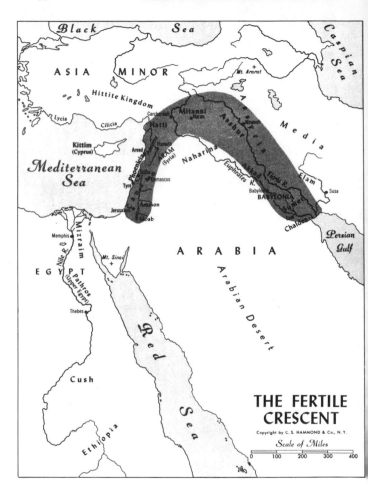

THE FERTILE CRESCENT

Copyright by C. S. HAMMOND & Co., N. Y.

Scale of Miles

0   100   200   300   400

courses in a generally southeastward direction
from their sources in the mountains of Armenia,
near Mount Ararat. They join to form the
Shatt-al-Arab about ninety miles north of the
Persian Gulf. The whole course of the Tigris to
its junction with the Euphrates is 1,146 miles.
The Euphrates traverses a longer course, of
about 1,800 miles.

Alluvium carried by the Tigris and Euphrates
made the soil of southern Mesopotamia (the
Greek word for the land between the rivers)
highly fertile. By 3000 B.C. this region was the
home of a non-Semitic people known as the Sumerians, who were responsible for some of the

This clay tablet, from southern Babylonia, is inscribed with an ancient map of the regions of the
world along with a cuneiform text above the map.

greatest cultural achievements in history. At the Sumerian city of Uruk (Biblical Erech, Gen. 10: 10) were found the oldest written records. The Sumerians used a stylus to inscribe characters on pieces of moist clay. The clay could then be baked in the sun or in a kiln to provide a permanent record. We call this system of writing *cuneiform.* It developed from early picture writing into a system in which wedge-shaped characters came to represent syllables. From these, words could be formed. The earliest cuneiform texts were records of business transactions in the Sumerian temples, but the writing system developed by the Sumerian scribes was adopted by their neighbors, the Semitic Akkadians, and by successive Babylonian, Assyrian, and even Hittite cultures. Although beginning as a utilitarian system for business purposes, cuneiform writing was quickly adapted for use in recording law codes, hymns, epic literature, and the whole gamut of written expression.

In addition to writing, the Sumerians gave us a mathematical system based on the number sixty, the "sexagessimal system" as it is called. Our sixty-second minute and 360 degree circle are based on this system. Sumerian law codes antedate the code of the Babylonian lawgiver Hammurabi.

Sumerian culture thrived during the millennium from 3000 B.C. to 2000 B.C. The Biblical

The Sumerian king list, in cuneiform, gives the earliest tradition of rulers who reigned before the Flood. The list also includes later rulers whose reigns reached to historical times.

The cuneiform text on this tablet records part of the Babylonian account of the Creation.

patriarch Abraham came upon the scene about the time that Sumerian culture was beginning to decline, soon to be replaced by that of the Babylonian lawgiver Hammurabi who was an Amorite.

At the time the Sumerians were developing their culture in the lower Tigris-Euphrates Valley, at the other end of the Fertile Crescent Egyptian civilization was developing in the Nile Valley and Delta. Egypt, too, produced a system of writing — the hieroglyphic characters that came to represent not only the object depicted but also syllables that could be combined with other syllables to form words. The cuneiform and hieroglyphic systems are not related, but the idea for such a writing system may have been brought to Egypt from Sumer. Because these writing systems were developed (we are indebted to those nineteenth century A.D. scholars who deciphered them), we now can understand much of the culture of the world of the Bible. The millennium from 3000 B.C. to 2000 B.C. saw the great pyramids built by the Egyptians in the desert west of the Nile. There, too, a variety of literature was produced. A political structure under the Pharaohs developed, and the arts and crafts flourished.

Herodotus agreed with other ancient historians in saying that Egypt was the gift of the Nile. The river valleys of Egypt and Mesopotamia

Egyptian sunk-relief in limestone. It depicts the head of a young man and dates from 1370 B.C.

provided an abundance of fertile soil, with the result that some workers could be spared for nonagricultural pursuits. Specialists in pottery, architecture, metalwork, weaving, and a variety of other occupations resulted. Also, a priestly class developed.

The ancients tended to believe that their arts and crafts were derived from their gods. Ptah, the Egyptian artisan god, had his forge at Memphis. The Bible, however, asserts that arts such as metallurgy and music developed in the line of Cain, Adam's son, who murdered his brother Abel (Gen. 4:19-23).

Whereas most of the Old Testament events took place in the Fertile Crescent lands, the Biblical world of the New Testament expanded to include a large part of Asia Minor, Greece, and Italy. Land travel, so common in the Old Testament, was augmented in New Testament times by sea travel. Since the Roman Empire controlled the entire Mediterranean and the lands that surrounded it, a missionary such as Paul could find easy access to the areas he felt called of God to evangelize.

2

THE LAND OF CANAAN

In modern times as in antiquity, many names arc given to the land on the Mediterranean's eastern seaboard, which was the home of the Israelites and their neighbors. The earliest Biblical records call it Canaan, the home of the Canaanites who were regarded as the descendants of Noah's grandson Canaan (Gen. 10:6, 15-19). After the Israelite conquest of the land, it became Israel, which was subsequently divided into two areas — Israel to the north and Judah to the south. Following the exile in Babylon we find the south called Judea and the area immediately to the north of Judea named Samaria, from the last capital of the northern kingdom. North of Samaria was Galilee.

From the Philistine inhabitants of the coastal plain the region was called "the land of the Philistines" (Exod. 13:17), or Palestine. The Romans called the area Syria Palestina, "Philistine Syria." More poetically it is often called

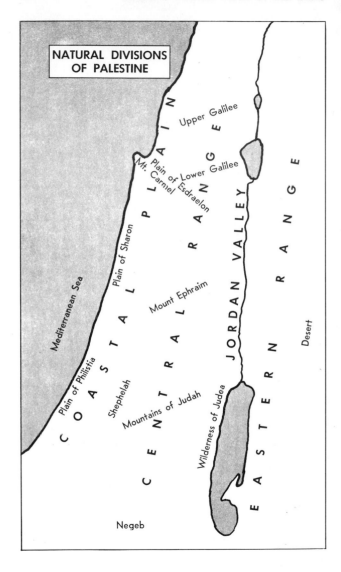

the Holy Land or the Promised Land. The Biblical promised land extended from Dan, at one of the sources of the Jordan in the north, to Beer-sheba, in the Judean Negev in the south. The area approximately matches that of the state of New Jersey. The highest point in Israel is Mount Hermon, 9,166 feet above sea level. The Dead Sea at Sodom is 1,286 feet below sea level — the lowest spot on earth.

Bordering the Mediterranean is a coastal plain lined with sand dunes and few good harbors. Jaffa served as a harbor for ancient Israel, but it is not used today. Haifa is modern Israel's chief port, but supplementary facilities are being developed at Ashdod, once an important Philistine city. South of Tel Aviv-Jaffa (the modern corporate name) was the Philistine Plain of Old Testament times. It is now called the Plain of Judea. Northward from Tel Aviv-Jaffa to Haifa, at the base of Mount Carmel, is the Plain of Sharon. The "rose of Sharon" (Song of Sol. 2:1) was considered particularly beautiful in ancient times. It is probably to be identified with the anemone. Today the famous Jaffa oranges are grown in the Plain of Sharon. North of Haifa the coastal plain broadens out to become the Zebulon Valley.

East of the coastal plain is a range of mountains extending the entire length of Israel. They average 2,000 feet in height and stretch two

hundred miles from Lebanon to Sinai. Access
to the central part of the country is through a
series of valleys. The largest and most important is the Esdraelon, which extends from modern Haifa past Megiddo to the Jordan Valley
which it joins at Beth-shan. The Esdraelon is
thirty miles in extent, and at its widest it is
twelve miles across. It has been used by traders
and warriors throughout recorded history.

North of Jaffa is the beginning of the Valley
of Aijalon, which passes the two Beth-horons
and Gibeon as it reaches the heart of the country. In this valley Joshua fought a battle against
a confederacy of kings from southern Canaan

Judean hills as they appear from the Jordan Valley
just south of Beth-shan.

The Sorek Valley. Today a road and railroad lead up the valley toward Jerusalem.

and, as recorded in the Book of Jashar, "the sun stood still" (Josh. 10:12-13).

South of the Aijalon Valley is the Valley of Sorek, which passes through the Samson country (Judg. 16:4). Timnah and Beth-shemesh are in the Valley of Sorek. The railroad from Haifa and Tel-Aviv to Jerusalem passes through the Sorek.

Still farther south is the Valley of Elah, or "The Valley of Terebinth Trees." This provides access from the coastal plain to the Hebron region. Above Socoh, a branch of the valley divides the lowlands, known as the Shephelah, from the Judean mountain range. Near the junction of the valley above Socoh, David met and killed the Philistine challenger Goliath (1 Sam. 17:1).

A valley known in the Bible as Zephathah (2 Chron. 14:10) has been identified with Wadi es-Safiyeh, which passes near Moresheth-gath, the birthplace of the prophet Micah (Mic. 1:1; 1:14).

The southern part of the Holy Land is the arid Negev (or Negeb). In its northern part, the Negev is an extension of the coastal plain. Eastward, it tilts up toward the cliffs and crags overlooking the Dead Sea and its southern extension, the Araba Valley. The western borders of the Negev are indistinguishable from the Sinai Peninsula.

Typical of the Negev region is this scene near the 4,000 year old site of Arad, about eighteen miles southeast of Hebron.

The climate of Palestine, like that of other Mediterranean lands, produces hot, dry summers and short winters. Such rain as falls comes in the winter. December, January, and February are the wettest months. From about June 15 to September 15 there is a total absence of rain. Since rainfall at best is marginal, it is appreciated when it comes, for the life it gives to otherwise barren fields. The average annual rainfall from 1931 to 1960 at Jerusalem in the Judean mountains was nineteen inches. At Beer-sheba, in the northern Negev, it was only eight inches, and at Eilat on the Gulf of Aqaba it was only one inch per year.

In the spring and at the end of the summer, a dry desert wind blows in from the east, making life miserable for a time. It usually lasts, however, just two or three days.

In Biblical times the most frequently mentioned produce of the land was wheat, grapes, figs, olives, and honey. Today, oranges and other citrus fruits are a major crop. Dates, bananas, avocados, guavas, and mangoes grow in the hot Jordan Valley and along the coastal plain.

Efforts are being made to replant the once extensive forests of the Holy Land. Indigenous trees include the Jerusalem pine, the tamarisk, and the carob. During the past century, eucalyptus trees have been introduced on a large scale.

More recently, pine forests have been planted in the mountains, and acacias on the dune lands of the Negev.

The wild flowers of the country include the hyacinth, crocus, and narcissus, which appear as early as December. They are followed by anemones, tulips, cyclamen, iris, and daisies. Among plants currently cultivated for domestic consumption and export are roses, gladioli, tulips, gerbera, and chrysanthemums. The sabra cactus, or prickly pear, is an indigenous fruit that can be seen growing wild along many of the country's roads.

Beasts of prey in modern Israel include hyenas, jackals, wildcats, lynx, otters, the mongoose, and the spotted weasel. Wolves and leopards appear in Galilee. Gazelles now are quite common, as are porcupines. The wild boar is hunted, but lions — frequently mentioned in the Bible — now are extinct in this part of the world. There are three species of hedgehog and several of shrew.

About four hundred species of birds have been identified in modern Israel. The Sea of Galilee continues to be rich in fish. Several areas, including a part of the former Lake Hula, have been designated as nature preserves. The Biblical Zoo in Jerusalem offers visitors an opportunity to see specimens of animal life mentioned in the Bible.

The standard of Ur, showing scenes of peace. Artifacts, records, and ruins uncovered at Ur, the birthplace of Abraham, reveal the complex civilization that existed before and during the time of the patriarch.

A shepherd and his sheep near Dothan. In this vicinity, along a main trade route, Joseph was cast into a pit and later sold by his brothers to a caravan of Midianites en route to Egypt.

A girl carrying bread at Hebron, a town in the
hill country of Judah. Here, at various times,
Abraham, Isaac, and Jacob pitched their tents.

Straw-laden donkeys near Petra, the rugged site
of the Old Testament Edomite capital, Sela.
Petra later became the main city of the Nabateans,
who were highly-skilled agriculturalists, traders,
and builders. The span of Nabatean civilization
included New Testament times.

An old Roman road affords a panorama of the
world's oldest city — Jericho, which is familiar
from both the Old and New Testaments, from the
conquest under Joshua to the healing of
Bartimaeus by Jesus.

Canyon walls of the wadi leading to En-gedi, the largest spring-fed oasis on the west shore of the Dead Sea. To the barren wasteland around En-gedi David retreated from King Saul's pursuit.

The Old City of Jerusalem, including the temple area with the Dome of the Rock, is majestically visible from the slopes of the Mount of Olives.

3

THE JOURNEYS OF THE PATRIARCHS

By 3000 B.C., the cultures of Egypt and Mesopotamia had flowered to the point where men had developed writing systems — hieroglyphic in Egypt and cuneiform among the Sumerians north of the Persian Gulf. Archaelogical discoveries made during the nineteenth and twentieth centuries enable us to see the Biblical records against the background of ancient Near Eastern history. We now can see Abraham as the heir to a great culture, a literate individual who conducted business in terms of the high civilization of his day.

The journeys of Abraham began at Ur (Gen. 11:31), one of the greatest of Sumerian cities, along the Euphrates River in southern Mesopotamia. Excavations at Ur show that the city was one of the most important in ancient Sumer. Objects of art and utility, dating about 2500 B.C., have been excavated at the Royal Cemeteries. Ur-Nammu, founder of the Third Dynasty of Ur — perhaps a century before Abraham — promulgated one of history's earliest law codes.

Abraham's journeys took him to Haran, a trading city in the region known as Padan-Aram, a name suggesting that the Arameans were already settled in the region. Laban, the father of Leah and Rachel, is specifically called a son of an Aramean (Gen. 28:5). From Haran, Abraham and his family journeyed southward to the land of Canaan, the home of different Semitic peoples who may be called, collectively, Canaanites (Gen. 12:5). During the Patriarchal Age, Canaan was under, at least nominal Egyptian control. The Patriarchs settled near major Canaanite cities such as Shechem, Bethel, and Hebron (Mamre). They lived a seminomadic life, living in tents, and they counted their wealth by the size of their flocks and herds. They used silver and gold as mediums of exchange. When Abraham purchased a burial site from Ephron the Hittite (Gen. 23: 16), he weighed out four hundred shekels of silver "according to the weights current among the merchants."

During a severe famine in Canaan, Abraham and his family went to Egypt. Canaan, modern Palestine or Israel, is watered by the rains of the fall, winter, and spring. Rainfall is never abundant and famine resulted in antiquity when rain

Street scene in Hebron, a familiar town in the Genesis accounts of the Patriarchs. It also served as King David's first capital.

Overlooking the Nile is the gigantic cliff temple of Abu Simbel, one of the many monuments built by Ramesses II.

was inadequate. The Book of Ruth tells of a later famine, when the family of Elimelech traveled to Moab in search of food.

Egypt, on the other hand, has practically no rainfall. The Nile River overflows its banks each summer as it bears the equatorial rains of Africa northward to the Mediterranean. The flood is looked upon as a great blessing, for without it Egypt would be but an extension of the Sahara Desert. Too much water, however, could do harm, destroying property and agricultural produce. Too little water could bring famine conditions to Egypt, as it did when Joseph was prime minister. Abraham hoped for food in Egypt when inadequate rain in Canaan caused drought conditions.

By Abraham's time, Egypt had experienced the early flowering of one of antiquity's great civilizations. Before 3000 B.C., the area south of the delta was united to the delta region to make the Egypt of the Pharaohs. Within a few centuries the first of the pyramids was erected and the Old Kingdom emerged as a period of great cultural advance. The Pharaoh was unchallenged god-king whose power was unlimited.

Both Sumer and Egypt, one in the Tigris-Euphrates Valley and the other in the Nile Valley, enjoyed the full light of civilization during the millennium preceding the Patriarchs of the Bible.

The period from about 2000 B.C. to 1600 B.C. saw the emergence of the Old Babylonian Empire in the region north of the Persian Gulf

Clay model of a sheep's liver, inscribed as a guide to Babylonian diviners. This model, found in southern Babylonia, dates from about 1700 B.C.

This section of the Beni Hasan tomb painting shows Semites entering Egypt during the nineteenth century B.C.

(formerly Sumer). The best known of the Old Babylonian rulers was Hammurabi, whose law code was discovered by the French at Susa in Iran (ancient Elam). Egypt was recovering from a period of chaos known as the First Intermediate (or Feudal) period, during the important Twelfth Dynasty, known as the Middle Kingdom. Tomb paintings from Bene Hasan depict Semitic traders entering Egypt. The arrival of Abraham must have looked much like the arrival of the Semites depicted at Bene Hasan. But before the age of the Patriarchs was over, Egypt was ruled by foreigners known as Hyksos.

4

INTO EGYPT AND BACK TO CANAAN

Egypt, the valley and the delta of the Nile, was geographically close to Canaan, and cultural contacts between the two areas were continuous. Semites entered Egypt from the dawn of history, leaving their imprint on the language of the country, which is of the Hamito-Semitic family, including both Hamitic and Semitic elements.

The career of Abraham included a trip to Egypt in a time of famine (Gen. 12:10-20). There was no food in Canaan, which is dependent on the rains for fertility; but Abraham realized that Egypt, which gets its moisture from the overflowing banks of the Nile at the time of the annual floods, likely had adequate food supplies. Abraham's visit in Egypt, however, was not a happy one. He tried to hide from the ruling Pharaoh the fact that Sarah was his wife. As a result, the Pharaoh took Sarah

Farming in the Delta region of the Nile. The river in the photo is a branch of the Nile River.

into his own harem, but the Egyptian ruler suffered the judgment of God for his sin. Abraham, Sarah, and all who were with them were forced to leave the country.

The fortunes of Israel were to be frequently associated with Egypt. Egyptian Pharaohs were ambitious to rule Canaan. With Egypt to the southwest and the lands of Babylonia and Assyria reached through routes heading northeast, Canaan (later Palestine or Israel) served as a land bridge for traders and soldiers.

Israel's longest experience in Egypt began in the days of Joseph and ended with the Exodus under Moses. Joseph, hated by his jealous brothers, was sold into slavery (Gen. 37:25-36).

Passing traders took him to Egypt where he became a trusted slave of an official of the Egyptian court named Potiphar (Gen. 39:1). Accused of attempted rape of Potiphar's wife, Joseph was imprisoned. While in jail, however, Joseph showed consideration for his fellow prisoners and wisdom in interpreting dreams. Later, he was asked to interpret the dreams of the Pharaoh, and prophesied a period of seven years of plenty, followed by seven years of famine (Gen. 41:25-36). The Pharaoh rewarded Joseph for this prophetic insight by making him second in authority over Egypt (Gen. 41:40). Under Joseph's wise administration, Egypt was spared the starvation that normally would follow years of drought. Joseph's brothers and father in Canaan learned that there was food in Egypt, and the brothers came to Egypt for food. There Joseph made himself known to his brothers, forgave them their earlier mistreatment of him, and urged that the entire family come to Egypt (Gen. 45).

The Israelites settled in the eastern Delta region of Egypt. This was fertile land where they would be able to tend their flocks. Life in the land of Goshen, as the region was called, was pleasant for the Israelite families during the lifetime of Joseph. His helpfulness in saving Egypt from the tragedies of famine was remembered and appreciated. The generation that settled in

Egypt died, but their children and grandchildren continued to prosper.

Many scholars feel that Israel entered Egypt during the time when a foreign dynasty — the Hyksos rulers — controlled the country. The foreign Israelites might well assume places of importance under other foreigners. Egyptian nationalism asserted itself, however, and we read of a new Egyptian dynasty arising with the goal of ridding the land of alien rulers. It was at this time that the presence of large numbers of Israelites was regarded as a threat to the security of the country. Egypt wanted to keep Israelites in the country as a slave labor force, but strenuous measures were taken to limit the population. When all else failed, the Egyptian ruler

Brickmaking in Eighteenth Dynasty Egypt (about 1450 B.C.). The painting is from the tomb of Rehkmire, Vizier of Upper Egypt.

Brickmaking in Egypt has not changed much through the centuries. The wet clay is poured into a wooden frame, which is lifted after the clay dries. Sun-dried bricks provide sturdy building material in a land of low annual rainfall.

decreed that male Israelite babies were to be thrown into the Nile River.

At this crucial time Moses was born (Exod. 2:1-9). Kept alive in a little boat — the familiar "basket . . . of bulrushes" (Exod 2:3) — Moses was adopted by Pharaoh's daughter and educated in the Egyptian court. In his mature years, however, Moses identified with his suffering people. After spending some years in the desert to the east as a refugee, he returned to Egypt to confront the Pharaoh and become the leader of the Exodus — the departure of the Israelites from Egyptian slavery.

Israelite slaves had labored on Pharaoh's store cities of Pithom and Raamses in the eastern Delta. From this area, following the institution of the Passover, the Israelites moved in

Prisoners brought into Egypt from countries to the north, as depicted on a bas-relief from the cliff temple built by Ramesses II.

the direction of the Sea of Reeds, somewhere in the area of the Bitter Lakes and Lake Timsah, north of the Gulf of Suez. Traditionally, the term "Red Sea" has been applied to the crossing point, but the term Red Sea is more properly applied to the large body of water to the south. The Hebrew *Yam Suf* is, literally, "The Sea of Reeds."

The crossing of the Sea of Reeds was regarded as a miracle. God caused a "strong east wind" to hold back the waters so that the Israelites could cross (Exod. 14:21-31). The pursuing Egyptian forces were drowned as the waters returned to their course. Israel, delivered out of Egypt, became a free people. They did not however, follow the coastal route directly into Palestine. That would have meant inevitable warfare with the Philistines, who were settling the southern coastal region of Palestine in force at this time. Instead, the Israelites turned southward into the Sinai Peninsula. At Mount Sinai God gave His Law to Moses, and the people pledged loyalty to their God. The priesthood was established, with Moses' brother, Aaron, serving as high priest. A movable shrine, the Tabernacle or Tent of Meeting, became the place of sacrifice and the despository for the tablets of the Law.

Camel riders ascend the slopes of Moses' Peak in Sinai.

From Sinai, Israel moved northward in the direction of Canaan — the Promised Land. At the border community of Kadesh-barnea spies were chosen and sent into the land. They brought back a report that the land was a good land, but that its inhabitants were strong and powerful (Num. 13:25-33). There seemed to be no hope that Israel could conquer the land, so plans of entry were abandoned. From Kadesh-barnea the people wandered with no distinct goal in view. The generation that left Egypt died in the wilderness. The pilgrims became wanderers. Caleb and Joshua survived, but even Moses died without entering the Promised Land (Deut. 34).

At the close of the "forty years" in the wilderness, a new plan of entry into Canaan was developed. Instead of entering from the south, the Israelites would go east, through the lands of Edom, Moab, and Ammon, and then cross the Jordan east of Jericho, thereby attacking the heart of the country.

This plan was followed. There were victories over kings east of the Jordan, such as Sihon and Og, and the Israelites finally reached the plains of Moab opposite Jericho. There Moses died, but Joshua had been appointed Moses' successor. Under Joshua the Israelites crossed the Jordan.

5

JOSHUA AND THE JUDGES

With the death of Moses, the mantle of leadership over the Israelite tribes fell to Joshua. Israel was in Trans-Jordan opposite the fortified Canaanite city of Jericho. Jericho held important strategic and psychological value. By pushing into Canaan from Jericho, Joshua could separate the city states of the south from those of the north, thus avoiding battle with a united Canaanite opposition.

After crossing the Jordan, Joshua and his armies camped near Jericho at an encampment known as Gilgal (Josh. 5:8-12). From Gilgal the campaign against Jericho was undertaken. After a seven-day siege Jericho fell, and the entire city was destroyed (Josh. 6). Only Rahab and her family were spared. Rahab had protected the spies sent by Joshua to Jericho, and they gave her their word that she and her household would be spared at the time the Israelites took Jericho.

The crossing of the Jordan and the fall of Jericho are presented in the Biblical text as miracles. God opened the waters of the Jordan as he had opened the Sea of Reeds to Israel at the time of the Exodus. Jericho, a strong Canaanite city, was taken by Israel only after divine intervention.

Victory at Jericho was followed by defeat at Ai (Josh. 7:1-5), now identified with et-Tel, two miles southeast of Bethel, up the road going northwestward from Jericho. The defeat at Ai was interpreted as God's judgment on Israel because a man named Achan had taken some of the spoil of Jericho that was to have been wholly devoted to the Lord. After Achan and his family had died for their sin, the armies of Joshua again fought at Ai. This time they were victorious.

The Jordan. Israel's crossing the Jordan under Joshua marked the end of forty years in the wilderness and the beginning of her life in Canaan.

General view of the oasis of Jericho, as seen from the site of the excavation of Old Testament Jericho.

Word of Joshua's victories reached the inhabitants of Canaan, and the men of Gibeon decided to seek a peaceful alliance with the Israelites (Josh. 9). Gibeon, modern el-Jib, is located about five and one-half miles from Jerusalem, a short distance to the west of the main road that heads northward toward Shechem and Samaria. The Gibeonites pretended to have traveled a great distance to the camp of Joshua, and they pursuaded him to make an alliance with them. Although the alliance was entered on the basis of trickery, Joshua considered it valid. He indicated that some of the Gibeonites would serve as menials who would chop wood and draw water for the "house of . . . God" (Josh. 9:23).

A confederation of Canaanite kings from the area south of Jerusalem determined to punish Gibeon for making peace with Joshua. Adoni-zedek of Jerusalem was leader of the coalition, which included the kings of the city-states of Hebron, Jarmuth, Lachish, and Eglon (Josh 10: 1-5). Faced with this threat, Gibeon sent to Gilgal to secure help from Joshua, and Joshua's army marched all night to reach Gibeon by morning. The result was a rout. Joshua pursued the southern confederacy through the pass

Stairs descending the pool at Gibeon. Such cisterns were common in ancient Palestine.

The Aijalon Valley where, following the miracle of Joshua's long day, the Israelite armies defeated a coalition of kings from southern Canaan.

of Beth-horon, reaching as far as Azekah and Makkedah. An ancient text known as the Book of Jashar (Josh. 10:13) tells how God supernaturally intervened, causing the sun to stand still until Joshua brought about the complete defeat of his foes. Following his successful defense of Gibeon, Joshua was in effective control of central and southern Canaan.

The final campaign described in the Book of Joshua was fought against a confederacy of kings from the northern part of Canaan under the leadership of Jabin of Hazor (Josh. 11). Hazor was excavated by Professor Yigael Yadin between 1955 and 1959. The site, covering 183 acres, lies north of the Sea of Galilee at the eastern foot of the mountains of Galilee where they slope down to the Jordan Valley. The battle was fought at the Waters of Merom (Josh. 11:7), perhaps to be identified with the Wadi Leimun near Meirun. Victory brought effective control of the north, but many areas were still contested, and it would be centuries before Israel would control all of its promised land. Jerusalem did not come under Israelite control until the reign of King David, and Gezer remained in enemy hands until Pharaoh, king of Egypt, conquered it and gave the town over to Solomon, his new son-in-law, as a wedding present (1 Kings 9:16).

During the time of the Judges, the Israelite tribes sought to consolidate their gains and deliver themselves from a series of oppressors. These were not times when a major power threatened to control western Asia. Egypt had passed the zenith of her power, and Assyria and Babylonia were yet to rise as formidable threats to the states of western Asia. The Philistines had occupied the coastal plain of southern Canaan where they formed a league of five cities: Ashdod, Ashkelon, Gaza, Gath, and Ekron. They were ethnically a part of the Indo-European "People of the Sea" who had left Crete and the Aegean region and attempted to invade Egypt. Repulsed by Pharaohs Merneptah and Ramesses III, they were successful in settling in south-

Stone serpent discovered at Gezer. The snake was an object of worship among the Canaanites.

At the Phoenician port city of Tyre, ruins from Roman times border an ancient Roman road that leads through an arch.

ern Canaan, where they gained control of the coastal plain, at about the same time the Israelites under Joshua were invading the hill country. Philistines and Israelites continued as rivals for many centuries.

Also at the same time, the Canaanites of the north, known as Phoenicians, developed into a seagoing people with major ports at Tyre and Sidon. The cedars of Lebanon provided timber for a shipbuilding industry, and Phoenician mariners were among the best in the Mediterranean. It was they who taught the Greeks the use of the alphabet. As a seagoing people, the

Phoenicians did not vie with the Israelites for territory as the Philistines did. At a later time, David and Solomon were on most friendly terms with the Phoenicians.

During the time of the Judges, the last major battle with the Canaanites occurred. Again a king of Hazor, named Jabin, was the foe. His general Sisera was leading the army in the Valley of Esdraelon when a sudden cloudburst

Cedars stand before a snow-streaked slope in Lebanon. Few mature specimens of the famed "Cedars of Lebanon" remain on the slopes that in ancient times were heavily forested.

caused his chariots to be mired in the mud. He escaped only to meet his death at the hand of a woman named Jael, the wife of Heber the Kenite (Judg. 5:24-31).

Other oppressors included the Moabites and the Ammonites east of the Jordan River and the Dead Sea. Moab and Ammon are described as descendants of Lot (Gen. 19:30-38). They were Semites, as were the Israelites, but they often were foes of Israel.

Erected on the site of the first and second temples, the Dome of the Rock in its present form dates back to A.D. 691. Repairs were undertaken in the sixteenth century and again in the 1960s.

Interior view of the Dome of the Rock.

The tomb of Cyrus at Pasargadae, which became
the capital of the Persian Empire during the
reign of Cyrus. Under Cyrus, captive peoples
including the Jews were permitted to return
to their homelands.

On this high mountain, near Bihistun (Bisitun),
the Persian ruler Darius the Great had his
autobiography carved in rock. The trilingual
inscription unlocked the Assyrio-Babylonian
system of cuneiform writing.

A street scene at Nativity Square in Bethlehem.
This famed village was the hometown of David
and the birthplace of Jesus.

A fruit vendor along a narrow street in
Nazareth. An open drain gutter runs along
the center of the street. This cosmopolitan Galilean
town was the scene of Jesus' boyhood days.

6

THE MONARCHY: SAUL, DAVID, AND SOLOMON

On the east side of the road going north from Bethel toward Shechem, within the territory of Ephraim, was Shiloh, the central shrine of the Israelite tribes after their settlement in Canaan. Here Eli the priest served, and here Hannah came with her prayer for a son (1 Sam. 1:10-11). After Samuel was born he was brought to Shiloh where he assisted the aging priest Eli. Samuel was to anoint Israel's first two kings.

When the people insisted on a king, Samuel was directed of God to anoint Saul, son of Kish, of the tribe of Benjamin (1 Sam. 10:1). Benjamin was a small tribe, and a king from Benjamin might not arouse the hostility of the larger tribes, particularly Judah and Ephraim. During Saul's early years he was successful in bringing victory to Israel over the Philistines and other enemies. Saul early showed signs of insanity, however, and his impulsive nature caused him to offer sacrifices when he should have waited for

The Judean wilderness. This scene is about half-way between Jerusalem and Jericho, not far from the old Jericho road.

Samuel. Convinced that Saul was disobedient to God, Samuel went to Bethlehem and anointed David, the youngest son of Jesse, to be king (1 Sam. 16:13).

The last years of Saul's life were tragic. Instead of fighting the Philistines, he exerted all his energies in an attempt to kill David. David fled to the Judean wilderness, the land to the east of Jerusalem, which remains barren and inhospitable to this day. David had the opportunity to kill Saul, but he refused to do so. Finally David fled to the Philistines where he served as a vassal of Achish of Gath (1 Sam. 27:3). Ironically, David was safer with his Philistines enemies than he was with his fellow Israelites.

Saul and his son Jonathan, who was a loyal friend of David, both died in a battle with the Philistines at Mount Gilboa in the Esdraelon Valley (1 Sam. 31). Another son of Saul, Ish-bosheth or Esh-baal, controlled much of the northern territory for a time, but David was acclaimed king of Judah at Hebron, south of Bethlehem (2 Sam. 2:11). After the death of Ish-bosheth, David's forces took the city of the Jebusites, which we now know as Jerusalem (2 Sam. 5:7). This centrally located city became David's capital. The Ark was brought up from Kirjath-jearim, and from the time of David to the present, Jerusalem has been the Holy City of the Jewish people.

With Israel united under David, the Philistines and other neighboring peoples could not hope to subdue this new powerful state. Internal problems arose, however. During his latter years David faced threats to his throne from

his son Absalom and from a man of Benjamin,
Saul's tribe, named Sheba. David's armies were
successful in maintaining his throne, but diffi-
culties were real. Famine and pestilence added
to the problems of David's last years (2 Sam.
21:1; 24:15).

Before David's death, two of his surviving
sons, Solomon and Adonijah, each found parti-
sans. Adonijah attempted to seize the throne
(1 Kings 1:5), but David designated Solomon
as his heir, and Adonijah fled for his life. Subsequently, Adonijah and a number of his par-
tisans were killed, and Solomon consolidated
power in his own name.

Solomon's many marriages were motivated in
large part by political and commercial consid-
erations. His foreign wives worshiped the gods
of their own countries, and idolatry became
rampant in Jerusalem.

One of Solomon's greatest achievements was
the building of the temple in Jerusalem (1 Kings
6). He also extended commercial and trade
activities, including sea routes from Ezion-geber,
near Elath, on the Gulf of Aqaba (1 Kings
9:26). Trade with Arabia, Africa, and India
was carried on in this way.

Toward the end of Solomon's reign signs of
trouble erupted. The Arameans and the Edomites broke away, refusing to pay their tributes
(1 Kings 11:14-25). The tax burden of the

Near Elat (ancient Elath) on the Gulf of Aqaba. The ancient site nearby, Ezion Geber, was a strategic seaport for Solomon in maintaining extensive trade with Africa and lands to the east.

A model of the town of Megiddo as it was in Solomon's day. A gateway to the Esdraelon Valley from the south, Megiddo was strategic both for military defense and trade.

Israelites was growing unbearable while the splendor of the court rivaled that of the greatest courts of the East. Solomon did not live to see the collapse of his kingdom, but it was not long in coming after his death.

7

THE DIVIDED KINGDOM: ISRAEL AND JUDAH

From the death of Solomon to the fall of Samaria was a period of two hundred years (922-722 B.C.). During that time the power structure of western Asia changed, and Assyria came to dominate the entire region.

Rehoboam, Solomon's son, hoped to succeed to the rule of the entire nation. His inflexibility, however, in the matter of tax relief was the breaking point. Jeroboam, the son of Nebat, who had fled from Solomon to Egypt, returned to lead the northern tribes in their quest for independence (1 Kings 12:12-16). Rehoboam could not prevent the secession of the north. Trade routes and the best agricultural lands were in the north. The fertile Esdraelon Valley was there. Judah held the more arid lands to the south. Efforts were made to prevent the secession, but the north continued as a separate state under a succession of dynasties. The south, Judah, maintained the Davidic dynasty throughout its history.

Jeroboam established his capital at Shechem, the city where Abraham first stopped when he entered the land of Canaan. Later kings moved the capital to Tirzah, and finally to Samaria, which remained as the capital of the northern kingdom until the Assyrian conquest. Religious shrines were established in the extreme north at Dan, near one of the sources of the Jordan River. Another shrine was located at Bethel, in the southern part of the kingdom of Israel. Judah's religious and political center remained at Jerusalem.

Under the Omri dynasty, Israel sought close relations with her Phoenician neighbors. Ahab, Omri's son, was married to Jezebel, a princess from Tyre who was a devotee to the Baal cult of that city (1 Kings 16:29-34). Although the north had forsaken the Jerusalem sanctuary, it still considered itself loyal to its God, Yahweh, even though He was worshiped at idolatrous shrines. Elijah and his successor, Elisha, were prophets of Yahweh, challenging Ahab and Jezebel to a showdown to determine who was to be the God of Israel. At Mount Carmel, above modern Haifa, the Baalists were unable to rouse Baal to their aid, but Elijah proved that Yahweh was the God who could answer by fire (1 Kings 18). Subsequently Jehu, with the aid of Elisha, seized control of Israel and determined to blot Baalism out of Israel

Baal, the storm god, holds a club in his right hand and a lance in his left hand. The lance extends upward in the form of a tree or stylized lightning. This relief was discovered at Ras Shamra.

(2 Kings 10:18-36). This, however, had repercussions in Israel's dealings with Phoenicia. Also, Jehu paid tribute to Shalmaneser III, the Assyrian king. The presentation of Jehu's tribute is recorded on the Black Obelisk of Shalmaneser.

Assyrian power continued to grow. Tiglath-pileser III moved westward and seized towns in

On this panel of the "Black Obelisk," Jehu, king of Israel, kneels and pays homage to Shalmanezer III, king of Assyria.

northern Israel. He took Reuben, Gad, and the half tribe of Manasseh, east of the Jordan, into exile (2 Kings 15:29). In 732 B.C., Damascus fell, and a decade later, shortly after the accession of Sargon of Assyria, Samaria fell (2 Kings 17:5-6). Its inhabitants were deported to other parts of the Assyrian Empire, and others from afar were brought in to repopulate Samaria and its environs. These new settlers became the Samaritans of later history. The tribes taken into exile had no continuing history. Some remnants certainly made their way south and continued to live among the people of Judah. The popular idea of the "lost tribes" stems from the fact that the exiles lost their identity.

From 722 to 587 B.C., Judah had to go it alone. She too was threatened by Assyria. Sennacherib tells how he took forty-six of the walled cities of Judah and shut up king Hezekiah "like a bird in a cage." Isaiah assured Hezekiah that Sennacherib would not enter Jerusalem, and the city was miraculously spared (Isa. 36-37).

Assyria, the scourge of western Asia, had troubles of her own. She was universally hated for her cruelties. Her end came when Cyaxeres the Mede joined forces with Nabopolassar of Babylon to destroy Assyria. Nebuchadnezzar was the young Babylonian prince leading the attack. In 614 B.C. the ancient capital at Ashur fell. Two years later the mighty Nineveh was destroyed so completely that its location was soon forgotten. In 610 B.C. Nebuchadnezzar

An Assyrian soldier beheads a captive, in a scene from the relief depicting Sennacherib's siege of Lachish, a fortified town in the lowlands of Judah.

Babylon according to artist Maurice Bardin. A bridge, set on boat-shaped piers, leads to a gate that forms part of the massive double wall that protected the city.

Dragon in glazed brick, from the Ishtar Gate of Babylon.

defeated the Assyrians at their last stronghold, in northern Mesopotamia at Haran — the city that Abraham had visited twelve centuries before. Pharaoh Necho of Egypt had determined to stop Nebuchadnezzar. He rightly felt that Babylon now was more of a threat than Assyria. Josiah of Judah marched his armies to Megiddo to stop Necho. Josiah was killed (2 Kings 23:29), but he may have delayed Necho long enough to assure Assyrian victory at Haran.

Nebuchadnezzar followed up his victories over Assyria with a victory over Egypt at Carchemish (609 B.C.). He might have moved southward toward the Egyptian border, but he learned that his father had died, and Nebuchadnezzar moved back to Babylon to secure the throne for himself.

Within a few years Nebuchadnezzar was back in western Asia. He laid claim to all the territory that had been subject to Assyria, and he

This brick uncovered at Babylon records the name and inscription of Nebuchadnezzar.

was determined to add still more territory. Jerusalem had withstood the siege of Sennacherib, but Nebuchadnezzar prepared to bring about its complete surrender. In 597 B.C. he defeated the armies of Judah and deported many of the leading inhabitants of Jerusalem (2 Kings 24:10-17). King Jehoiachin was taken to Babylon, as was the prophet Ezekiel and many other leaders of Judah.

Jeremiah, remaining behind in Judah, urged his people to accept in good grace the fact that the Babylonians were now their rulers. A pro-Egyptian party, however, urged rebellion. Nebuchadnezzar returned in 587 B.C. He took and destroyed Jerusalem with its temple, ushering in the period of history known as the Exile, or the Babylonian captivity (2 Kings 25:8-21).

8

THE EXILE AND THE RETURN

Unlike the Assyrians who transported their captives to new areas, breaking up the family and tribal units, the Babylonians permitted their exiles to maintain their community life in new surroundings. Jewish communities sprang up in Babylon. Ezekiel lived in such a community along the River Chebar, perhaps the "Grand Canal" (Ezek. 1:1). Although far from their temple, the Jewish community did gather together for prayer and the study of the Scriptures. Some entered business and prospered in Babylon.

When Cyrus of Anshan came to the throne, he began the series of conquests that created the Persian Empire. With the fall of Babylon, the policy of Cyrus was enunciated permitting captive peoples to return to their lands. Under a leader named Shesh-bazzar, later replaced by Zerubbabel, the first company of exiles made their way back to Jerusalem (Ezra 2). Later,

Tribute-bearing Babylonians and Syrians, from a relief on the stairway of the Apadana at Persepolis, a capital of the Persian Empire.

Ezra the scribe returned with another company of Jews (Ezra 8).

In addition to the hardships of the journey, these pioneers faced hostility from the people of the land. Since the Babylonians did not settle new peoples in the Jerusalem area, Samaritans, Edomites, and other neighboring peoples had hoped to claim some of this land for themselves. The edict of Cyrus provided the legal claims of the Jews to the land, and later kings recognized it as binding. Guerilla warfare was practiced, however, so that the builders needed to carry a

The gate of Xerxes at Persepolis, with guardian man-headed bulls at the eastern doorway.

The southeast corner of the Jerusalem Old City wall. Under the Persians, Jewish exiles returned to restore the walls and rebuild the temple at Jerusalem.

sword for defense in one hand while they built with the trowel in the other hand.

Those who returned first set up an altar on the old temple site. Discouragements caused the work of rebuilding the temple to be delayed, but finally the new structure was dedicated among scenes of people rejoicing. This second temple, later embellished by Herod the Great, was to stand until the armies of Titus would destroy it in A.D. 70.

9

ALEXANDER AND HIS SUCCESSORS IN THE BIBLE LANDS

Under the Persians, the Jews developed their institutions and, under ruling high priests, enjoyed a semiautonomus status. The Persians apparently thought highly of the Jews and even employed them as mercenary soldiers at such remote places as Elephantine, at the first cataract of the Nile River.

The map of Asia was to be changed by Alexander of Macedon, the next world conqueror. Leaving his home in Macedonia, Alexander crossed into Asia Minor, following the coast of the Mediterranean. He determined to take all of the Mediterranean coastal cities, thus preventing the Persians from using their fleet. Tyre resisted, with the result that Alexander had his men build a causeway to join the mainland to the island city. Pressing on, Alexander reached Egypt where he was acclaimed a son of Ammon, hence a legitimate Pharaoh. Returning to western Asia, Alexander pushed relentlessly onward

Silver drachma of Alexander the Great. The coin
was found in Persepolis.

until he took all the major cities of the Persian
Empire, reaching at last the banks of the Indus
in the Punjab region of India. Anxious to go
farther, Alexander could not do so because his
troops desired to return to their homes after
eleven years of wandering and warfare. On the
way back, Alexander died at Babylon.

Following the death of Alexander, his gen-
erals fought over the succession. One, named
Ptolemy, emerged as ruler of Egypt, and another,
Seleucus, took most of the Asiatic portion of the
empire, including Syria and Babylon. Palestine
was ruled by the Ptolemies during the early
Ptolemaic period, but in 201 B.C. Antiochus III

defeated Egypt at Panion, and Palestine became part of the Seleucid Syrian Empire.

Under Antiochus IV (Epiphanes) an attempt was made to force Hellenistic ways upon the Jews. The observance of Judaism was forbidden, and a statue of Zeus was placed in the Jerusalem temple. An aged priest, Mattathias,

Pottery jug filled with thirty-five silver tetradrachmas, probably from a private bank of a citizen of Shechem in the second century B.C. Bearing images of Syrian Greek rulers, the coins span a minimum of ninety years, from at least 285-193 B.C.

rebelled against these Hellenizing policies and, with his sons, he began to wage guerilla warfare. When Mattathias died, his son Judah (Greek Judas), surnamed the Maccabee, became leader of the revolt.

Dynastic struggles in Syria helped the Jewish cause, and ultimately the Jews were victorious. An independent Jewish state emerged under a dynasty of rulers known as the Hasmoneans. They acquired considerable territory until partisan fighting brought in the Romans under Pompey (63 B.C.). From this time on Judea was a part of the Roman Empire.

10

HERODIAN AND NEW TESTAMENT PALESTINE

The Palestine of Herodian and New Testament times comprised several provinces. Judea, to the south, was basically the Old Testament territory of the tribe of Judah. Judea was the most orthodox portion of the country, and its inhabitants had a feeling of pride in their adherence to traditional Judaism. The temple aristocracy was of the party known as the Sadducees, a party that had come to terms with the Hellenistic way of life.

North of Judea was Samaria, the home of the Samaritans, who were descendants of the population settled in the area at the time that Assyria deported the people of the northern kingdom. The Jews looked upon the Samaritans as a half-breed people who had rejected the Jerusalem temple in favor of one of their own on Mount Gerizim, near Nablus (the Grecianized word, "New City," for earlier Shechem). The temple on Mount Gerizim had been destroyed in the

early days of the Hasmonean dynasty, but the
Samaritans clung to their holy mountain, as
remnants of the Samaritans still do today. Generally, Jews and Samaritans avoided contact with
one another, a taboo that Jesus broke (John
4).

Still farther north was the province of Galilee,
an area which had been incorporated into the

On the top of Mount Gerizim, Samaritans assemble
annually to celebrate the Passover.

A replica of the famed Pilate Inscription stands at Caesarea, where the original was discovered. For protection, the original inscription was taken to Jerusalem.

in the vicinity of the Sea of Galilee. Tradition says that the Sermon on the Mount was spoken on a mountain near Capernaum, in the same region.

The climax of Jesus' ministry, leading to His death and resurrection, took place in Jerusalem and its environs. The home of Mary and Martha was in Bethany, around the southern slope of the Mount of Olives. From the top of the Mount of Olives, Jesus ascended after His death at Calvary and burial in a nearby tomb.

veterans from Alexander's armies who settled there. One of the cities bore the name Pella, the home town of Alexander in Macedonia.

South of Judea was Idumea, the Greek form of the Old Testament word *Edom,* the home of the Edomites. Edomites had been pushed out of their old lands south and east of the Dead Sea by the Nabatean Arabs, who developed a high culture in this generally barren territory.

Most of the ministry of Jesus was in Galilee. All of his disciples, except Judas, were Galileans. Many of His miracles were performed

Carved in red sandstone is the facade of El-Khazneh, the Treasury, near the entrance of the Siq (a narrow gorge) that leads to the basin of Petra.

Jerash, in Trans-Jordan, where extensive Roman ruins mark a busy, commercial Decapolis city in New Testament times. These columns form part of the west wing of the Forum. The lighter color at the base of the columns indicate the depth of earth removed by excavators.

Nazareth, where Jesus spent His boyhood days. The village is nestled in hills rising above the Esdraelon Valley.

Jewish state about a century before the time of Jesus. It was called, "Galilee of the gentiles." Judeans noted the peculiar accent of the Galileans, and they despised the city of Nazareth with the rhetorical question, "Can anything good come out of Nazareth?" (John 1:46).

East of the Jordan was the region known as Perea, roughly equivalent to Trans-Jordan. Jews often would cross from Galilee to Perea and go down the east bank of the Jordan to avoid the necessity of passing through Samaria.

The Decapolis was a league of Hellenistic cities comprising in part the Greek-speaking

11

THE JOURNEYS OF PAUL

The missionary statesman Paul, formerly Saul of Tarsus, was a citizen of a city in Asia Minor that had famous schools and a position of prestige as the residence of the governor of Cilicia. From Tarsus, Saul came to Jerusalem, where he studied under a renowned teacher of the Pharisees named Gamaliel. Before his conversion Saul was an ardent persecutor of the church. After his encounter with the risen Christ, Saul — who now used his Roman name Paul — became the most active Christian evangelist.

Paul and his companions sailed from Seleucia, the port of Antioch, for Cyprus, after which they went to Perga in Pamphylia in southern Asia Minor. During three journeys, Paul evangelized most of western Asia Minor, Macedonia, and Greece.

The first missionary journey saw Paul at Iconium, Lystra, and Derbe in the provinces of Pamphylia and Galatia (Acts 13-14). On the

Antioch of Syria, the home base for Paul's missionary journeys. Its church sent delegates to the Jerusalem conference recorded in the Book of Acts.

second journey he again visited the churches he had established there, and then moved westward to Troas from where he sailed to Macedonia. After ministering at Neapolis, Philippi, Thessalonica, and Berea, in Macedonia, he journeyed southward to Greece where he preached at Athens and Corinth. Before returning home he ministered at Ephesus, a major city in western Asia

Minor, where the shrine of Artemis (Diana) was located (Acts 16-18).

On his third journey, again Paul traveled through southern Asia Minor, retracing many of the paths he had trodden before. From Ephesus he went north to Troas, then across the Aegean to Macedonia and Greece (Acts 18-21). His return voyage followed the Aegean coast of Asia Minor, then to the island of Rhodes, Patara in Lycia, the Phoenician city of Sidon, and finally through Tyre, Ptolemais, and Caesarea to Jerusalem.

Paul's last journey was his voyage to Rome (Acts 27). This time he was a prisoner, taken

Marble Street at Ephesus was part of the scene familiar to Paul because of his intensive ministry among the Ephesian Christians.

Along the old Appian Way, leading to Rome, Paul completed his final journey before imprisonment and martyrdom.

to the capital of the empire to stand trial. The voyage began at Caesarea, the seat of government for Roman Palestine. Following the coast of Phoenicia and Asia Minor, the vessel stopped briefly at Fair Havens on the southern shore of Crete. Continuing westward, the ship encountered stormy weather and was wrecked. Paul and his companions used boards and broken pieces of the ship as life rafts, reaching Malta (Melita) with no loss of life.

From Malta, Paul took another boat that passed through Syracuse in Sicily, landing at Puteoli in Italy. From there he traveled overland on the old Appian Way to Rome.

12

THE CHURCHES OF ASIA MINOR

Missionary activity was not limited to Paul's effort, and the first century saw numerous churches developing throughout the Roman Empire. Best known from the New Testament are the seven churches of Proconsular Asia, described in the Book of Revelation in chapters 2 and 3.

Ephesus was the capital of the province that comprised southwestern Asia Minor. Its impressive ruins are a major tourist attraction today.

Sardis, capital of the gold-rich country of Lydia at an earlier time and seat of government after the Persian conquest, was one of the most important cities of the area. The walls of a Christian church, erected before the fourth century of the Christian era, have been discovered immediately outside the pagan temple of Artemis, built in the fourth century B.C. Sardis had a major Jewish community, which probably provided the nucleus for the church there.

Smyrna is the only one of the seven cities that remains a major city in modern Turkey. Known now as Izmir, it is a major seaport and boasts an international airport as well.

Pergamum, or Pergamos, was once the capital of a kingdom ruled by a dynasty of kings

The altar of Zeus at Pergamum, to which the apostle John probably referred when he spoke of "Satan's Throne." This reconstructed model stands in the State Museum at Berlin.

bearing the name Attalus. In 133 B.C. Attalus III bequeathed his property to the Romans, who annexed his territory, incorporating it into the Province of Asia with Pergamum as its capital. A shrine to Aesculapius, the god of medicine, was erected outside the city.

Thyatira, on the road from Pergamos to Sardis, was famed as a center for the dyeing of purple (cf. Acts 16:14). It has left few remains.

Philadelphia, about twenty-seven miles southeast of Sardis, is still inhabited. Some of the ancient walls, with remains of a temple and other buildings, are still standing.

Laodicea, about fifty-six miles east-southeast of Izmir, was the seat of a medical school in ancient times. Powder for the cure of the eye

General view of the Asclepium at Pergamum.

disease known as ophthalmia was manufactured there. The city also was known for the manufacture of cloth and garments from the black wool of sheep raised in the area. Ruins of ancient Laodicea can be seen near the Turkish city of Denizli.

13

SINCE NEW TESTAMENT TIMES

At the close of the New Testament, Christianity was a persecuted but growing faith. Paul and others had carried the gospel to the far reaches of the Roman Empire. Some had been martyred for their faith, but Christianity met the needs of mankind in a way that the older paganism could not. Especially among the poorer classes of Romans, the Christian message found a ready audience.

By the fourth century, Christians had made such an impact that the emperor Constantine accepted Christianity. Persecution stopped as Christianity first became a legal religion and later the official religion of the empire. With a new capital at Byzantium, now called Constantinople (modern Istanbul), the Christian faith in its official form was considered essential to good citizenship. Unhappily this included the persecution of both non-Christians and nonconforming Christians.

Chapel of the Ascension on the Mount of Olives. The dome is Islamic, but the lower part of the structure is of Crusader architecture — a good example of the various cultural influences upon the face of Palestine.

When Mohammed's followers left Arabia with the new faith of Islam in the seventh century, they found many Christians who were so disgruntled with Byzantium that they looked upon the Moslems as friends and deliverers. The Coptic Church of Egypt put up little resistance. It had suffered too much at the hand of the Byzantines.

The rapid spread of Islam meant that Christianity ceased to be the major faith in large parts of the Near East and North Africa. The transition from paganism to Christianity went another step — that from Christianity to Islam. Eventually this became the status of most of

The past still meets the present at the Pool of the Sultan, just outside the walls of the Old City of Jeresalem. Here animals are traded and sold every Friday.

Ruins of a Crusader castle at Sidon harbor. For more than two centuries, the Crusaders fought the Moslems in the Near East. Ruins of their castles still can be seen today.

Syria and Palestine, North Africa, and Turkey. Islam also entered Europe, but by that time its force was spent. After successes in Spain, Moslems (and Jews) were expelled, with rather sad results for Spain itself.

European rulers were encouraged to march armies eastward to rescue the holy places from the "infidels." The resulting movement, the Crusades, brought eastern lands temporarily into Christian hands, but the crusaders never became a part of the country. They ruled the land as medieval fiefdoms. Christian institutions were introduced with some lasting results, but Saladin and his Moslem armies succeeded in driving the crusaders out of Palestine.

Seljuk and Ottoman Turks invaded the area, but they adopted the Moslem faith, and consequently the religious situation was not changed. With World War I came the defeat of the Turkish Empire and the division of the Near East into spheres of influence. The British were assigned the mandate for Palestine, and the French controlled Syria. Movements for independent

A scene at the "Shepherds' Fields" by Bethlehem. People wearing both traditional and modern dress are common sights in Palestine.

Interior view of the Golden Gate, Jerusalem. A remnant of barbed wire symbolizes the division and conflict that marked the Holy City's recent past.

statehood developed both among the Arabs of the area and the Jews who had been promised a national homeland in Palestine in the Balfour Declaration of Britain during World War I.

With the establishment of the State of Israel in 1948, the Bible lands have been the scene of three major wars and continuing antagonism between the Jewish state and her Arab neighbors. There is bitter irony in the fact that the land of the Prince of Peace could be so given over to hate and warfare. Humanly speaking, no end of the problem is in sight, but "with God all things are possible" (Matt. 19:26).

BIBLIOGRAPHY

Albright, W. F. *Archaeology and the Religion of Israel.* Baltimore: Johns Hopkins Press, 1942.

_____. *The Archaeology of Palestine.* Harmondsworth, Middlesex England: Penguin Books, 1954.

_____. *From the Stone Age to Christianity.* Baltimore: Johns Hopkins Press, 1946.

Barton, G. A. *Archaeology and the Bible.* Philadelphia: American Sunday School Union, 1937.

Burrows, Millar. *What Mean These Stones?* New Haven: American Schools of Oriental Research, 1941.

Kenyon, Kathleen M. *Archaeology in the Holy Land.* 3d ed. New York: Praeger Publishers, 1970.

Frank, Harry Thomas. *Bible Archaeology and Faith.* Nashville: Abingdon Press, 1971.

Pfeiffer, Charles F. ed. *The Biblical World.* Grand Rapids: Baker Book House, 1966.

Pritchard, James B. *The Ancient Near East in Pictures Related to the Old Testament.* Princeton: Princeton University Press, 1954.

_____. *Archaeology and the Old Testament.* Princeton: Princeton University Press, 1958.

Wright, G. E. *Biblical Archaeology.* 2d ed. Philadelphia: Westminster Press, 1957.

INDEX

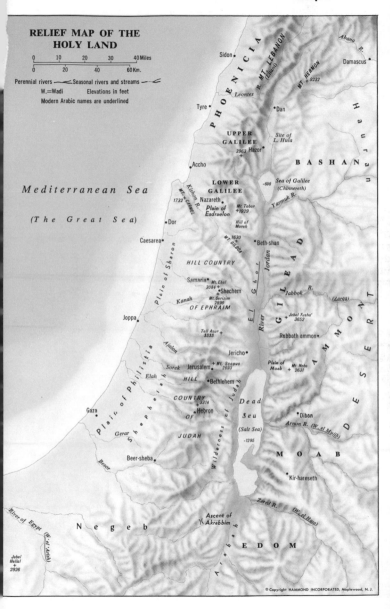

Map 1

RELIEF MAP OF THE
HOLY LAND

0   10   20   30   40 Miles
0   20   40   60 Km.

Perennial rivers ——— Seasonal rivers and streams ——<
W.=Wadi   Elevations in feet
Modern Arabic names are underlined

Mediterranean Sea

(The Great Sea)

Abana R.

Sidon

Damascus

PHOENICIA

R. MT. LEBANON (Litani)

MT. HERMON × 9232

Leontes

Tyre

Dan

Hauran

UPPER GALILEE
3963 Hazor +

Site of L. Hula

Accho

BASHAN

LOWER GALILEE
-698

Sea of Galilee (Chinnereth)

Nazareth

Mt. Tabor +1929

MT. CARMEL 1732

Kishon R.

Plain of Esdraelon

Hill of Moreh

Yarmuk R.

Dor

+1630 MT. GILBOA

Beth-shan

Caesarea

El Ghor

Jordan River

GILEAD

Jabbok R.

(Zarqa)

HILL COUNTRY

Plain of Sharon

Samaria

Mt. Ebal 3084

Shechem

Mt. Gerizim 2890

Jebel Yusha' 3652

Kanah

OF EPHRAIM

Joppa

AMMON

Rabbath ammon

Tell Asur +3333

Ajalon

Jericho

Sorek

Jerusalem

+ Mt. Scopus 2693

Plain of Moab

Mt. Nebo +2631

Elah

HILL

Bethlehem

COUNTRY
+3314

Gaza

Gerar

Shephelah

OF

Hebron

Dead Sea
(Salt Sea)
-1295

Dibon

Plain of Philistia

JUDAH

Wilderness of Judah

Arnon R. (W. el Mujib)

Besor

Beer-sheba

MOAB

Kir-haresuth

River of Egypt (W. el-Arish)

Negeb

Ascent of Akrabbim

Zared R. (W. el Hasa)

Jebel Hellal × 2926

EDOM

Arabah

© Copyright HAMMOND INCORPORATED, Maplewood, N. J.

Map 2

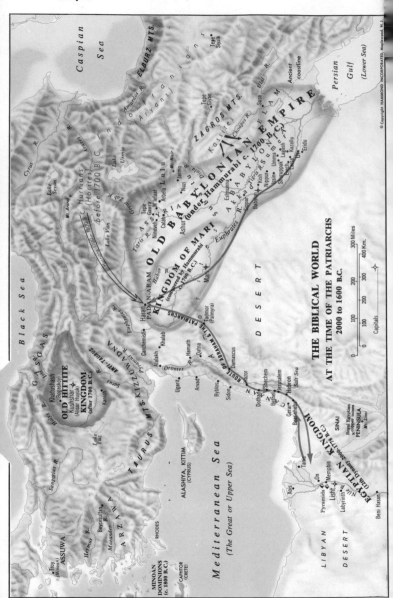

THE BIBLICAL WORLD
AT THE TIME OF THE PATRIARCHS
2000 to 1600 B.C.

Map 3

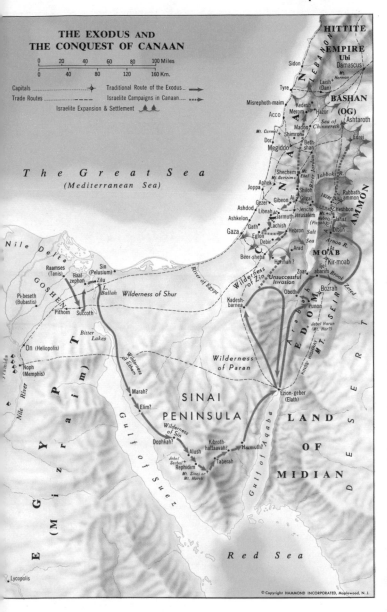

THE EXODUS AND THE CONQUEST OF CANAAN

| 0 | 20 | 40 | 60 | 80 | 100 Miles |
| 0 | 40 | 80 | 120 | 160 Km. |

Capitals ....✦
Trade Routes ....
Israelite Expansion & Settlement 🌲🌲

Traditional Route of the Exodus ➝
Israelite Campaigns in Canaan ⇢⇢

The Great Sea
(Mediterranean Sea)

HITTITE EMPIRE
Ubi
Damascus
Mt. Hermon

Sidon

Tyre

Misrephoth-maim
Kedesh
Merom
Acco
Madon
Hazor
Laish (Dan)
BASHAN (OG)
Ashtaroth
Shimron
Sea of Chinnereth
Mt. Carmel
Dor
Megiddo
Beth-shan
Edrei
Madon

Shechem
Mt. Ebal
Mt. Gerizim
River Jordan
Jabbok R.

Aphek
Joppa
Shiloh
Ai
Gibeon Gilgal
Jazer
Rabbath-ammon
AMMON

Gezer
Jericho
Heshbon
Ashdod
Libnah
Jarmuth
Jerusalem
Mt. Nebo (Pisgah)
Jahaz
Ashkelon
Gath
Lachish
Dibon
Gaza
Eglon
Debir
Hebron
Salt Sea
Arad
Beer-sheba
Hormah?
MOAB
Kir-moab
Zoar
Ije-abarim
Arnon R.
Brook Zered

Wilderness of Zin
Unsuccessful Invasion
Kadesh-barnea
Oboth
Bozrah
EDOM
MT. SEIR
Jebel Harun (Mt. Hor?)
Punon
Kings Highway

Nile Delta

Raamses (Tanis)
Baal-zephon
Sin (Pelusium)
Wilderness of Shur
River of Egypt
Pi-beseth (Bubastis)
Pithom
Succoth
Zilu
L. Ballah

On (Heliopolis)
Bitter Lakes
Wilderness of Etham

Noph (Memphis)
Pyramids

GOSHEN

E G Y P T
(Mizraim)

Nile River

Gulf of Suez

Wilderness of Sin
Dophkah?
Alush
Rephidim
Jebel Serbal
Mt. Sinai or Mt. Horeb
Taberah
Kibroth-hattaavah?
Hazeroth?

SINAI PENINSULA

Wilderness of Paran

Marah?
Elim?

Ezion-geber (Elath)

Gulf of Aqaba

Arabah

LAND OF MIDIAN

DESERT

Red Sea

Lycopolis

© Copyright HAMMOND INCORPORATED, Maplewood, N.J.

Map 4

THE TWELVE TRIBES
IN CANAAN

0   10   20   30   40 Miles
0   20   40   60 Km.

The Great Sea

Damascus
Abana R.

Sidon
Zarephath
Leontes R.
MOUNT LEBANON
MT. HERMON
Phoenicians

Tyre
Abel-beth-maachah
Laish or Leshem (Dan)
D A N
Kanah
En-hazor
Kedesh
B a s h a n
Hammon
Iron
Misrephoth-maim
Achzib
Abdon
Beth-emek
Ramah
Hazor
Acco
Achshaph
Cabul
Hukkok
Chinnereth
Karnaim
Ashtaroth
Aphek
Kishlon
Rimmon
Madon
Sea of Chinnereth
G e s h u r
Aphek
Golan?
Argob
Hannathon
Shimron
Gath-hepher
Hammath
Haroseth
Jokneam
Sarid
En-dor
Jabneel
Yarmuk R.
Havoth-jair
Edrei
Dor
Plain of Jezreel
Mt. Tabor
Chesulloth
Camon
M A N A S S E H
Megiddo
ISSACHAR
Jezreel
Shihor-libnath
Taanach
Mt. Gilboa
Harod (Spring)
Beth-shan
Pella
Ramoth-gilead
Dothan
Ibleam
Jabesh-gilead
Bezek
Tirzah?
Thebez
Abel-meholah
The Great Sea
MANASSEH
Shechem
Zaphon
Mahanaim
A M M O N
Mt. Ebal
Mt. Gerizim
Taanath-shiloh
Succoth
Jabbok R.
Pirathon
Tappuah
Ianohah
Penuel
Mizpeh
Plain of Sharon
Kanah
Aphek
Lebonah
Shiloh
Adam
Gath-rimmon?
Bene-berak
EPHRAIM
Ataroth
Betonim
Jogbehah
Joppa (Japho)
Ono
Timnath-serah
Naarath
Jazer
Rabbath-ammon
Lod
Lower Beth-horon
Ophrah
Ai
Mizpah
Beth-nimrah
Jabneel
Gezer
Bethel
Ramah
Jericho
Gilgal
Abel-shittim
Elealeh
Ekron
Gibbethon
Gibeon
Geba
Kiriath-jearim
BENJAMIN
Beth-jeshimoth
Heshbon
Ashdod
Sorek
Zorah
Gibeah
Mt. Nebo
Eltekeh
Timnah
Jebus (Jerusalem)
Baal-meon
Medeba
Ashkelon
Makkedah
Beth-shemesh
Jarmuth
Bethlehem
R E U B E N
Libnah
Azekah
Etam
Tekoa
Ataroth
Jahaz
Gath
Mareshah
Keilah
Beth-zur
Kiriathaim
Dibon
Gaza
Eglon
Lachish
J U D A H
Hebron
En-gedi
Arnon R.
Aroer
Gerar
Debir
Ziph
C a l e b
Carmel
Ziklag
Anab
Eshtemoh
Madmannah
Jattir
Arad
Beer-sheba
Moladah
Ai?
Salt Sea
Sharuhen
Hormah
Kenites
M O A B
Raphia
Beth-palet?
Aroer
Kir-hareseth
Cherethites
S I M E O N
Brook Zered
Rehoboth
Ascent of Akrabbim
E D O M
D A N
A S H E R
N A P H T A L I
Z E B U L U N
G A D
G i l e a d

© Copyright HAMMOND INCORPORATED, Maplewood, N.

Map 5

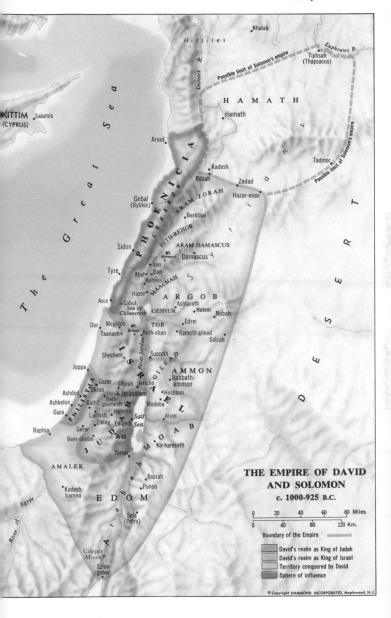

THE EMPIRE OF DAVID
AND SOLOMON
c. 1000-925 B.C.

0   20   40   60   80 Miles
0   40   80   120 Km.

Boundary of the Empire

David's realm as King of Judah
David's realm as King of Israel
Territory conquered by David
Sphere of influence

© Copyright HAMMOND INCORPORATED, Maplewood, N.J.

Map 6

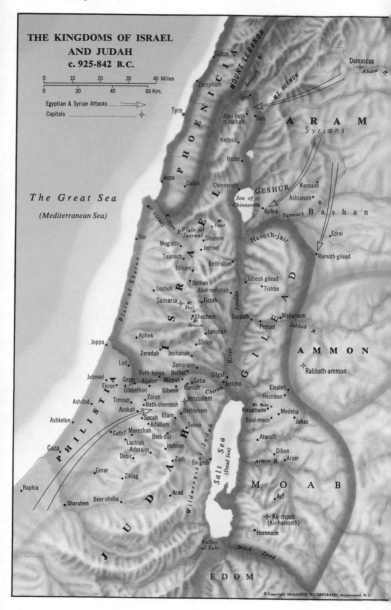

THE KINGDOMS OF ISRAEL AND JUDAH
c. 925-842 B.C.

0   10   20   30   40 Miles
0   20   40   60 Km.

Egyptian & Syrian Attacks →
Capitals ⊹

The Great Sea
(Mediterranean Sea)

PHOENICIA

Sidon
Zarephath
Tyre
MOUNT LEBANON
Litani R.
Ijon
Abel-beth-maachah
Dan
Kedesh
Hazor
MT. HERMON
Damascus
Abana R.
ARAM
Syrians

Acco
Cabul
Chinnereth
GESHUR
Sea of Chinnereth
Karnaim
Ashtaroth
Aphek
Yarmuck R.
Bashan

Dor
Mt. Carmel
Kishon R.
Mt. Tabor
Plain of Jezreel
Shunem
Megiddo
Jezreel
Taanach
Ibleam
Beth-shan
Havoth-jair
Edrei
Ramoth-gilead

Plain of Sharon
ISRAEL
Dothan
Abel-meholah
Jabesh gilead
Tishbe
Samaria
Mt. Ebal
Tirzah
Shechem
Mt. Gerizim
Janohah
Shiloh
Succoth
Penuel
Mahanaim
Jabbok R.
GILEAD

Joppa
Aphek
Zeredah
Jeshanah
Jordan River
AMMON

Lod
Zemaraim
Bethel
Jabneel
Beth-horon
Mizpah
Geba
Gilgal
Rabbath-ammon
Ekron
Gezer
Aijalon
Ramah
Jericho
Gibbethon
Gibeon
Cherith
Elealeh
Heshbon
Zorah
Jerusalem
Mt. Nebo
Kiriathaim
Timnah
Beth-shemesh
Bethlehem
Baal-meon
Medeba
Ashdod
Azekah
Socoh
Etam
Tekoa
Jahaz
Ashkelon
Gath?
Adullam
Beth-zur
Mareshah
Hebron
Ataroth
Lachish
Adoraim
Dibon
Gaza
Debir
Ziph
En-gedi
Arnon R.
Aroer
PHILISTIA
Salt Sea
(Dead Sea)
Gerar
Ziklag
Arad
Wilderness of Judah
MOAB
Raphia
Beer-sheba
Ar?
Sharuhen
JUDAH
Kir-moab
(Kir-haraseth)
Horonaim
Valley of Salt
Brook Zered

EDOM

© Copyright HAMMOND INCORPORATED, Maplewood, N.J.

Map 7

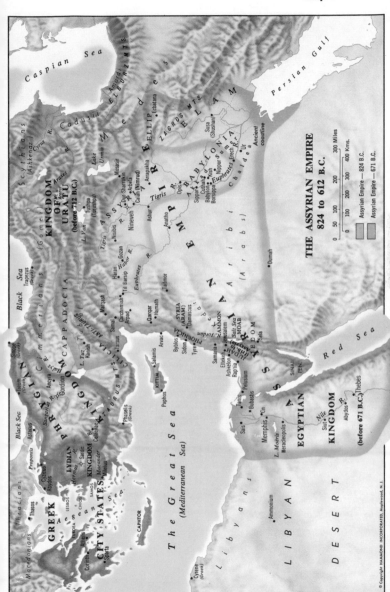

THE ASSYRIAN EMPIRE
824 to 612 B.C.

| | 0 | 50 | 100 | 200 | 300 Miles |
| | 0 | 100 | 200 | 300 | 400 Kms. |

Assyrian Empire —824 B.C.
Assyrian Empire —671 B.C.

© Copyright HAMMOND INCORPORATED, Maplewood, N.J.

Map 8

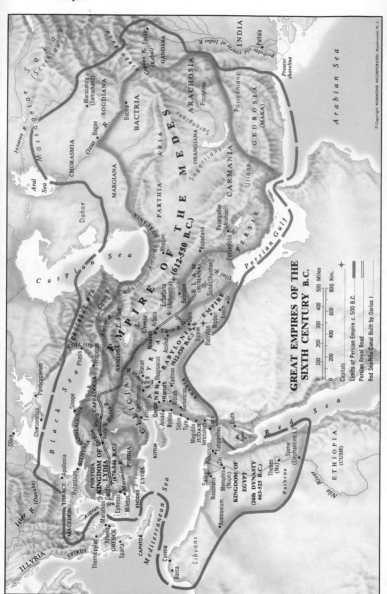

GREAT EMPIRES OF THE
SIXTH CENTURY B.C.

Map 9

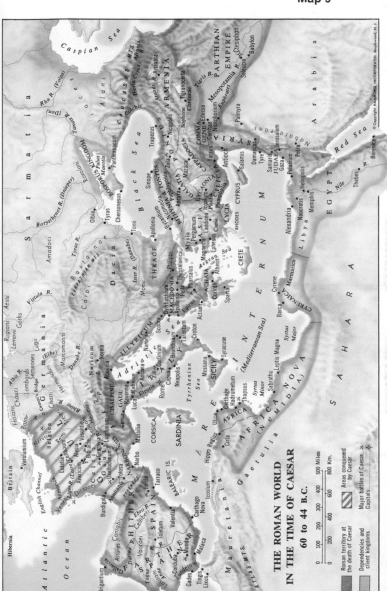

THE ROMAN WORLD
IN THE TIME OF CAESAR
60 to 44 B.C.

Roman territory at
the death of Caesar

Dependencies and
client kingdoms

Areas conquered
by Caesar

Major battles of Caesar. ×
Capitals............●

0   100   200   300   400   500 Miles
0   200   400   600   800 Km.

© Copyright H.M.CO. INCORPORATED, Maplewood, N.J.

Map 10

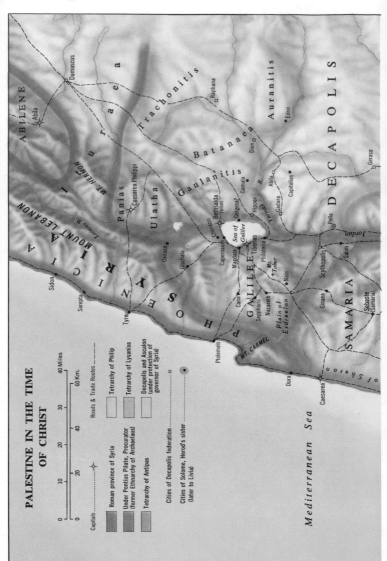

PALESTINE IN THE TIME
OF CHRIST

0	10	20	30	40 Miles
0	20	40	60 Km.	

Capitals ✦

Roman province of Syria

Under Pontius Pilate, Procurator
(former Ethnarchy of Archelaus)

Tetrarchy of Antipas

Tetrarchy of Philip

Tetrarchy of Lysanias

Decapolis and Ascalon
under protection of
governor of Syria

Roads & Trade Routes

Cities of Decapolis federation ☐

Cities of Solome, Herod's sister
(later to Livia) ⊙

Mediterranean Sea

ABILENE
Damascus
Abila

PHOENICIA
MOUNT LEBANON
MT. HERMON
Leontes R.

ITURAEA
Trachonitis
Raphana

Batanaea
Auranitis
Edrei
Dion

Sidon
Sarepta

Panias
Caesarea Philippi
Ulatha
Gaulanitis

Cadasa
Chorazin
Bethsaida
Julias
Gergesa?

Gischala
Capernaum
Hippos
Gamala

Sea of Galilee

DECAPOLIS
Gerasa
Capitolias
Abila
Gadara
Pella

Tyre
Magdala
Tiberias
Philoteria
Yarmuk R.

Cana
GALILEE
Mt. Tabor

Jordan R.

Sepphoris
Nazareth
Nain

Ptolemais
MT. CARMEL
Plain of Esdraelon

Scythopolis
Salim

SAMARIA
Ginaea
Sebaste
Samaria

Dora
Plain of Sharon

Caesarea

Map 11

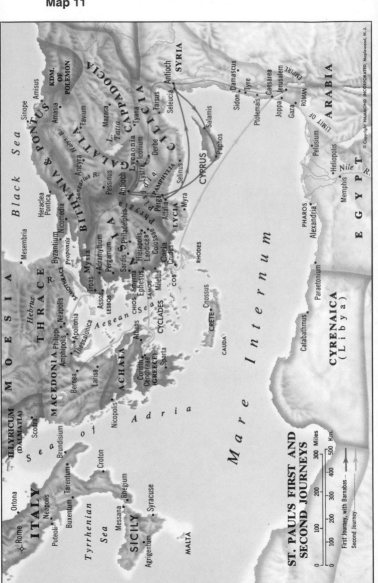

ST. PAUL'S FIRST AND
SECOND JOURNEYS

First Journey, with Barnabas ----
Second Journey ----

Map 12

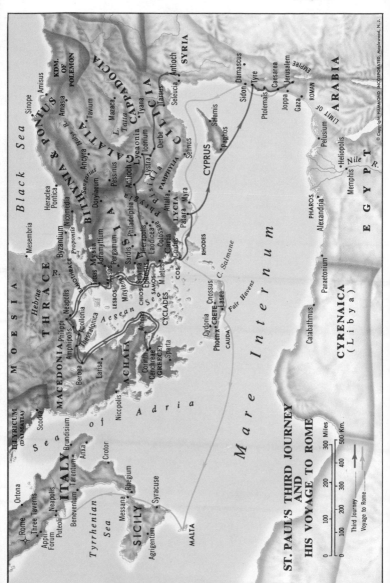

ST. PAUL'S THIRD JOURNEY
AND
HIS VOYAGE TO ROME

	Miles	
0	100	200	300 Miles
0	100 200 300	400	500 Km.

Third Journey

Voyage to Rome

Map 13

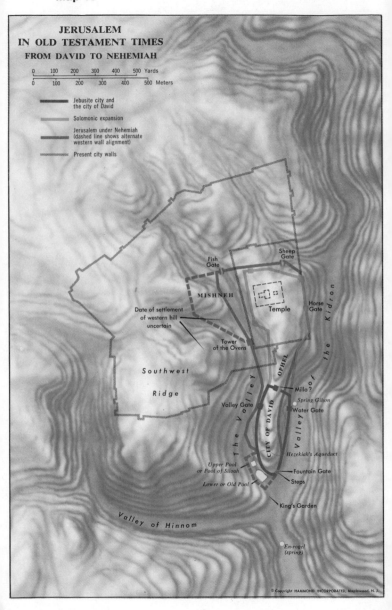

JERUSALEM
IN OLD TESTAMENT TIMES
FROM DAVID TO NEHEMIAH

| 0 | 100 | 200 | 300 | 400 | 500 | Yards |
| 0 | 100 | 200 | 300 | 400 | 500 | Meters |

Jebusite city and
the city of David

Solomonic expansion

Jerusalem under Nehemiah
(dashed line shows alternate
western wall alignment)

Present city walls

Fish
Gate

Sheep
Gate

MISHNEH

Temple

Horse
Gate

Date of settlement
of western hill
uncertain

Tower
of the Ovens

OPHEL

Valley of the Kidron

Southwest

Ridge

Millo?

Spring Gihon

Valley Gate

Water Gate

The Valley

CITY OF DAVID

Valley of the Kidron

Hezekiah's Aqueduct

Upper Pool
or Pool of Siloah

Fountain Gate

Lower or Old Pool

Steps

King's Garden

Valley of Hinnom

En-rogel
(spring)

© Copyright HAMMOND INCORPORATED, Maplewood, N. J.

Map 14

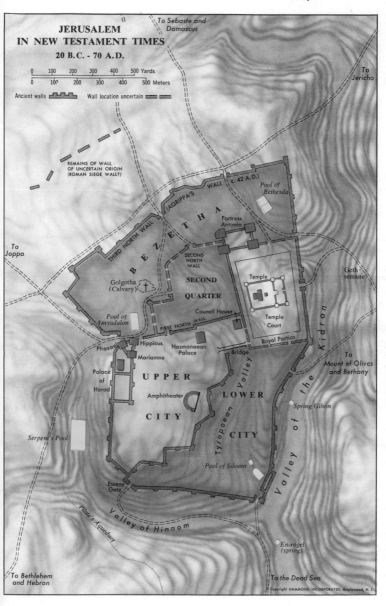

JERUSALEM
IN NEW TESTAMENT TIMES
20 B.C. - 70 A.D.

0 100 200 300 400 500 Yards
0 100 200 300 400 500 Meters

Ancient walls   Wall location uncertain

To Sebaste and
Damascus

To Jericho

REMAINS OF WALL
OF UNCERTAIN ORIGIN
(ROMAN SIEGE WALL?)

(AGRIPPA'S) WALL c. 42 A.D.

THIRD NORTH WALL

BEZETHA

Pool of
Bethesda

Fortress
Antonia

SECOND
NORTH
WALL

SECOND
QUARTER

Golgotha
(Calvary)

Temple

Temple
Court

To
Joppa

Pool of
Amygdalon

Council House

FIRST NORTH WALL

Royal Portico

Phasael

Hippicus

Hasmonaean
Palace

Bridge

Geth-
semane

Mariamne

To
Mount of Olives
and Bethany

Palace
of
Herod

UPPER
CITY

Amphitheater

LOWER
CITY

Spring Gihon

Valley of the Kidron

CITY

Tyropoean Valley

Serpent's Pool

Pool of Siloam

Essene
Gate

Pilate's Aqueduct

Valley of Hinnom

En-rogel
(spring)

To Bethlehem
and Hebron

To the Dead Sea

Copyright HAMMOND INCORPORATED, Maplewood, N. J.

Map 15

CARDINAL BERAN LIBRARY
ST. MARY'S SEMINARY

3 3747 00028 1896

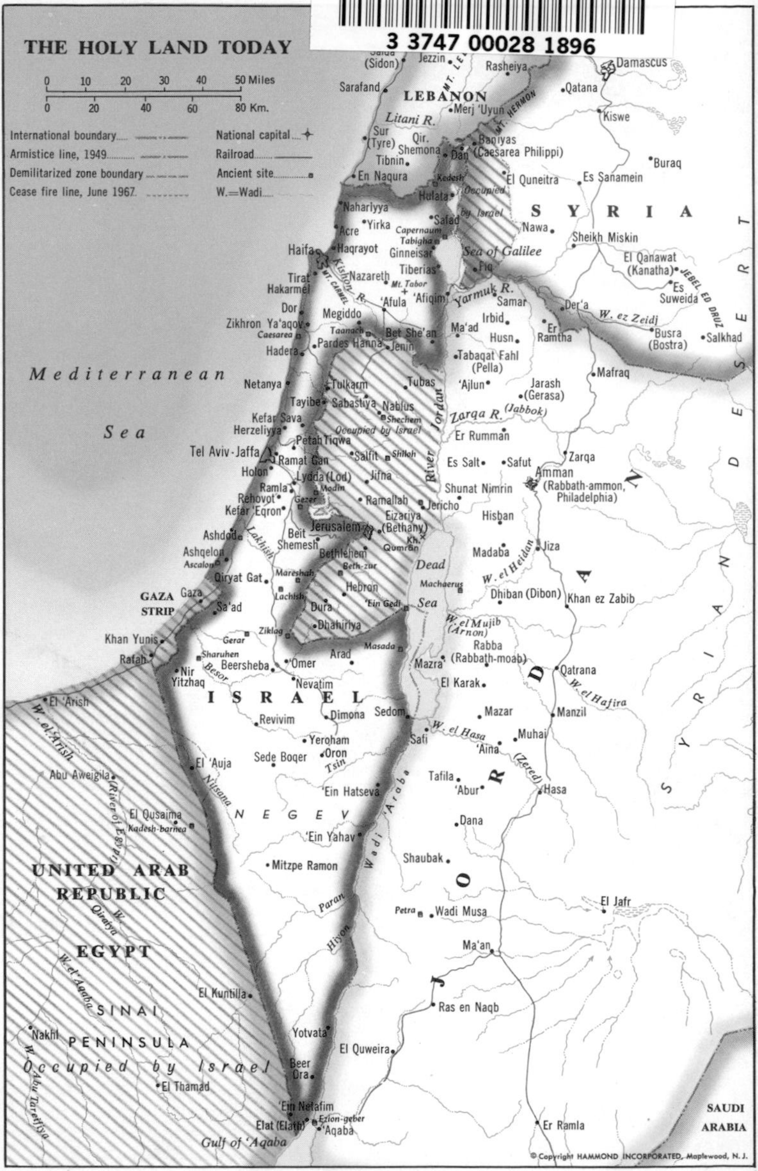

THE HOLY LAND TODAY

0	10	20	30	40	50 Miles
0	20	40	60		80 Km.

International boundary _____ National capital _+_
Armistice line, 1949 _____ Railroad _____
Demilitarized zone boundary _____ Ancient site _____
Cease fire line, June 1967 _____ W.=Wadi

© Copyright HAMMOND INCORPORATED, Maplewood, N.J.